LIGHT AND THREAD

LIGHT
AND
THREAD

HAN KANG

Translated by Maya West
and e. yaewon & Paige Aniyah Morris

HOGARTH
LONDON/NEW YORK

Hogarth
An imprint of Random House
A division of Penguin Random House LLC
1745 Broadway, New York, NY 10019
randomhousebooks.com
penguinrandomhouse.com

This work was originally published in Korean as 빛과 실, or *Bichgwa
Sil,* by Munhak and Jisungsa Co., Ltd, Seoul, South Korea in 2025,
copyright © 2025 by Han Kang. This translation is published
in the United Kingdom by Hamish Hamilton, an imprint of
Penguin Random House UK, London.

Hardcover ISBN 979-8-217-15503-3
Ebook ISBN 979-8-217-15504-0

Printed in the United States of America

1st Printing

First U.S. Edition

BOOK TEAM: Production editor: Jennifer Rodriguez • Managing editor:
Rebecca Berlant • Production manager: Linnea Knollmueller •
Copy editor: Taylor McGowan • Proofreaders: Claire Maby,
Deborah Bader, Amy Brosey

Book design by Susan Turner

The authorized representative in the EU for product safety and
compliance is Penguin Random House Ireland, Morrison
Chambers, 32 Nassau Street, Dublin D02 YH68, Ireland.
https://eu-contact.penguin.ie

CONTENTS

A NOTE ON THE TRANSLATIONS

The Nobel Lecture "Light and Thread" is translated
by e. yaewon and Paige Aniyah Morris. Maya West
translated the rest of the book.

LIGHT AND THREAD

ast January, while sorting through my storeroom ahead of an imminent move, I came across an old shoe box. I opened the box to find several diaries dating back to my childhood. Among the stack of journals, there was a pamphlet, the words "A Book of Poems" written in pencil across its front. The booklet was thin: five sheets of rough A5 paper folded in half and bound with staples. I had added two zig-zagging lines under the title, one line progressing up in six steps from the left, the other inclining down in seven steps to the right. Was it a kind of cover illus-tration? Or simply a doodle? The year—1979—and my name were written on the back of the chapbook, with a total of eight poems inscribed on the inner leaves by the same neat, penciled hand as on the front and back covers. Eight different dates marked the bottom of each page in chronological order. The lines penned by my eight-year-old self were suitably innocent and unpolished, but one poem from April caught my eyes. It opened with the following stanzas:

Where is love?
It is inside my thump-thumping beating chest.

What is love?
It is the gold thread connecting between our hearts.

In a flash I was transported back forty years, as memories of that afternoon spent putting the pamphlet together came back to me. My short, stubby pencil with its biro-cap extender, the eraser dust, the big metal stapler I had sneaked out from my father's room. I remembered how after learning that our family would be moving to Seoul, I had an impulse to gather the poems I had scribbled on slips of paper, or in the margins of notebooks and workbooks, or between journal entries, and collect them into a single volume. I recalled, too, the inexplicable feeling of not wanting to show my "Book of Poems" to anyone once it was completed.

Before placing the diaries and the booklet back as I had found them and closing the lid over them, I took a photo of that poem with my phone. I did this out of a sense that there was a continuity between some of the words I had written then and who I now

4

was. Inside my chest, in my beating heart. Between our hearts. The golden thread that joins—a thread that emanates light.

Fourteen years later, with the publication of my first poem and then my first short story in the following year, I became a Writer. In another five years, I would publish my first long work of fiction, which I had written over the course of about three years. I was, and remain, intrigued by the process of writing poetry and short stories, but writing novels has a special pull on me. My books have taken me anywhere from a year to seven years to complete, for which I have exchanged considerable portions of my personal life. This is what draws me to the work. The way I can delve into, and dwell in, the questions I feel are imperative and urgent, so much so that I decide to accept the tradeoff.

Each time I work on a novel, I endure the questions, I live inside them. When I reach the end of these questions—which is not the same as when I find answers to them—is when I reach the end of the writing process. By then, I am no longer as I was when I began, and from that changed state, I start again. The next questions follow, like links in a chain, or like dominoes, overlapping and joining and continuing, and I am moved to write something new.

While writing my third novel, *The Vegetarian,* from 2003 to 2005, I was staying with some painful questions: Can a person ever be completely innocent? To what depths can we reject violence? What happens to one who refuses to belong to the species called human?

Electing not to eat meat in a refusal of violence, and in the end declining all food and drink except water in the belief that she has transformed into a plant, Yeong-hye, the protagonist of *The Vegetarian,* finds herself in the ironic situation of quickening towards death in her bid to save herself. Yeong-hye and her sister In-hye, who are in fact co-protagonists, scream soundlessly through devastating nightmares and ruptures, but are together in the end. I set the final scene in an ambulance, as I hoped Yeong-hye would remain alive in the world of this story. The car rushes down the mountain road beneath blazing green leaves while the alert older sister gazes intensely out the window. Perhaps awaiting a response, or perhaps in protest. The entire novel resides in a state of questioning. Staring and defying. Waiting for a response.

Ink and Blood, the novel that followed *The Vegetarian,* continues these questions. To refuse life and the world in order to refuse violence is an impossibility. We cannot, after all, turn into plants. Then how do we continue on? In this mystery novel, sentences in roman and italic type jostle and clash, as the main character, who has long wrestled with death's shadow, risks her life to prove that her friend's sudden death cannot have been by suicide. As I wrote the closing scene, as I described her dragging herself across the floor to crawl her way out of death and destruction, I was asking myself these questions: Must we not survive in the end? Should our lives not bear witness to what is true?

With my fifth novel, *Greek Lessons,* I pushed even further. If we must live on in this world, which moments make that possible? A woman who has lost her speech and a man who is losing his sight are walking through stillness and darkness when their solitary paths cross. I wanted to attend to the tactile moments in this story. The novel progresses at its own slow pace through stillness and darkness to when the woman's hand reaches out and writes a few words in the man's palm. In that luminous instant that expands to an eternity, these two characters reveal the softer parts of themselves. The question I wanted to ask here was this: Could it be that by regarding the softest aspects of humanity, by caressing the irrefutable warmth that resides there, we can go on living after all in this brief, violent world?

Having reached the end of this question, I began thinking about my next book. This was in the spring of 2012, not long after *Greek Lessons* was published. I told myself I would write a novel that takes another step towards light and warmth. I would suffuse this life- and world-embracing work with bright, transparent sensations. I soon found a title and was twenty pages into the first draft, when I was forced to stop.

I realized that something within was preventing me from writing this novel.

Until then, I hadn't considered writing about Gwangju.

I was nine years old when my family left Gwangju

in January 1980, roughly four months before the mass killings began. When I happened across the upside-down spine of *Gwangju Photo Book* on a bookshelf a few years later and looked through it when there were no adults around, I was twelve. This book contained photographs of Gwangju residents and students killed with clubs, bayonets, and guns while resisting the new military powers that had or-chestrated the coup. Published and distributed in se-cret by the survivors and the families of the dead, the book bore witness to the truth at a time when the truth was being distorted by strict media suppression. As a child, I hadn't grasped the political significance of those images, and the ravaged faces became fixed in my mind as a fundamental question about humans: Is this the act of one human towards another? And then, seeing a photo of an endless queue of people waiting to donate blood outside a university hospital: Is this the act of one human towards another? These two questions clashed and seemed irreconcilable, their incompatibility a knot I couldn't undo.

So that one spring day in 2012, as I tried my hand at writing a radiant, life-affirming novel, I was once again confronted by this unresolved problem. I had long lost a sense of deep-rooted trust in humans. How, then, could I embrace the world? I had to face this impossible conundrum if I meant to move forwards, I realized. I understood that writing was my only means of getting through and past it.

I spent the better part of that year sketching out my novel, imagining that May 1980 in Gwangju would form one layer of the book. In December, I visited the cemetery in Mangwol-dong. It was well past noon and a heavy snow had fallen just the day before. Later, as the light darkened, I walked out of the freezing cemetery with my hand over my chest, close to my heart. I told myself this next novel would look squarely at Gwangju, rather than consigning it to a single layer. I obtained a book containing more than 900 testimonials, and every day for nine hours over the course of a month, I read each account collected there. Then I read up on not just Gwangju but other cases of state violence. Then, looking even further afield and back in time, I read about mass killings that humans have repeatedly perpetrated throughout the world and throughout history.

During this period of researching my novel, two questions were often foremost in my mind. Back in

my mid-twenties, I had written these lines on the
first page of every new diary:

> *Can the present help the past?*
> *Can the living save the dead?*

As I continued reading, it became clear that
these were impossible questions. Through this sus-
tained encounter with the bleakest aspects of humanity, I felt the remnants of my long-fractured belief
in humanity shatter entirely. I all but gave up on the
novel.

Then I read the diary entries of a young night-
school educator. A shy, quiet youth, Park Yong-jun
had participated in the "absolute community" of self-
governing citizens that formed in Gwangju over the
ten-day uprising in May 1980. He was shot and killed
in the YWCA building near the provincial adminis-
tration headquarters where he had chosen to remain,
despite knowing that the soldiers would be returning
in the early hours. On that last night, he had written
in his diary, "Why, God, must I have a conscience
that pricks and pains me so? I wish to live."

Reading these sentences, I knew with the clarity

of lightning which way the novel must go. And that my two questions had to be reversed.

Can the past help the present?
Can the dead save the living?

Later, as I was writing what would become *Human Acts,* I sensed at certain moments that the past was indeed helping the present, and that the dead were saving the living. I would revisit the cemetery from time to time, and somehow the weather would always be clear. I would close my eyes, and the sun's orange rays would suffuse my lids. I felt it as life's own light. I felt the light and air envelop me in indescribable warmth.

The questions that remained with me long after I saw that book of photographs were these: How are humans this violent? And yet how is it that they can simultaneously stand opposite such overwhelming violence? What does it mean to belong to the species called human? To negotiate an impossible way through the empty space between these two precipices of human horrors and human dignity, I needed the assistance of the dead. Just as in this novel,

Human Acts, the child Dong-ho tugs at his mother's hand to coax her towards the sun.

Of course, I could not undo what had been done to the dead, to the bereaved, or to the survivors. All I could do was lend them the sensations, emotions, and life pulsing through my own body. Wishing to light a candle at the start and the end of the novel, I set the opening scene in the municipal gymnasium where the bodies of the deceased were housed and the funeral services were held. There, we witness fifteen-year-old Dong-ho laying white sheets over the bodies and lighting candles. Staring into the pale blue heart of each flame.

The Korean title of this novel is *Sonyeon-i onda.* The last word "onda" is the present tense of the verb "oda," to come. The moment the sonyeon, the boy, is addressed in the second person as *you,* whether the intimate or the less intimate *you,* he awakens in the dim light and walks towards the present. His steps are the steps of a spirit. He draws ever nearer and becomes the now. When a time and place in which human cruelty and dignity existed in extreme parallel is referred to as *Gwangju,* that name ceases to be a proper noun unique to one city and instead becomes a common noun, as I learned in writing this book. It comes to us—again and again across time and space, and always in the present tense. Even now.

When the book was finally completed and published in the spring of 2014, I was surprised by the pain that readers confessed to feeling while reading it. I had to take some time to think about how the pain I had felt throughout the writing process and the distress that my readers had expressed to me were connected. What might be behind that anguish? Is it that we want to put our faith in humanity, and when that faith is shaken, we feel as though our very selves are being destroyed? Is it that we want to love humanity, and this is the agony we feel when that love is shattered?

Does love beget pain, and is some pain evidence of love?

That same year in June, I had a dream. A dream in which I was walking across a vast plain as a sparse snow was falling. Thousands upon thousands of black tree stumps dotted the plain, and behind every last one of them was a burial mound. At some point, I was stepping in water, and when I looked back, I saw the ocean rushing in from the edge of the plain, which I had mistaken for the horizon. Why were there graves in a place like this? I wondered. Wouldn't all the bones in the lower mounds closer to the sea have been swept away? Shouldn't I at least relocate the bones in the upper mounds, now, before it was too late? But how? I didn't even have a shovel.

The water was already up to my ankles. I awoke, and as I stared out of the still-dark window, I intuited that this dream was telling me something important. After I wrote the dream down, I recall thinking that this might be the start of my next novel.

I didn't have a clear idea of where it might lead, however, and found myself starting and scrapping the beginnings of several potential stories I imagined might follow from that dream. Finally, in December 2017, I rented a room on Jeju Island and spent the next two years or so dividing my time between Jeju and Seoul. Walking in the forests, along the sea, and on the village roads, feeling the intense Jeju weather at every moment—its wind and light and snow and rain—I sensed the outline of the novel come into focus. As with *Human Acts,* I read testimonies from massacre survivors, pored over materials, and then, in as restrained a manner as I could without looking away from the brutal details that felt almost impossible to put into words, I wrote what became *We Do Not Part.* The book was published nearly seven years after I had dreamed of those black tree stumps, that surging sea.

In the notebook I kept while working on that book, I made these notes:

> *Life seeks to live. Life is warm.*
> *To die is to grow cold.*
> *To have snow settle over one's face rather than melt.*
> *To kill is to make cold.*

> *Humans in history and humans in the cosmos. The wind and the ocean currents. The circular flow of water and air that connects the entire world. We are connected. I pray that we are connected.*

The novel is made up of three parts. If the first part is a horizontal journey that follows the narrator, Kyungha, from Seoul to her friend Inseon's home in the Jeju uplands through heavy snow towards the pet bird she has been tasked with saving, then the second part follows a vertical path that leads Kyungha and Inseon down to one of humanity's darkest nights— to the winter of 1948 when civilians on Jeju were slaughtered—and into the ocean's depths. In the third and final part, the two light a candle at the bottom of the sea.

Though the novel is pulled forwards by the two friends, just as they take turns holding the candle, its true protagonist and the person linked to both Kyungha and Inseon is Inseon's mother, Jeongsim. She who, having survived the massacres on Jeju, has fought to recover even a fragment of her loved one's bones so that she can hold a proper funeral. She who refuses to stop mourning. She who bears pain and stands against oblivion. Who does not bid farewell. In attending to her life, which had for so long seethed with pain and love of an equal density and heat, I think the questions I was asking were these: To what extent can we love? Where is our limit? To what degree must we love in order to remain human to the end?

Three years on from the publication of the Korean edition of *We Do Not Part,* I have yet to complete my next novel. And the book I imagined would follow that next one has been waiting on me for a long time. It is a novel that is formally linked to *The White Book,* which I wrote out of a wish to lend my life, for a brief time, to my older sister who left the world a mere two hours after she was born, and also to peer into the parts of us that remain indestructible no matter what. As always, it's impossible to predict when anything will be completed, but I will go on writing, however slowly. I will move past the books I've already written and continue on. Until I round a corner and find that they're no longer in my line of sight. As far into the distance as my life allows.

As I move away from them, my books will continue their lives independently of me and travel according to their own destinies. As will those two sisters, together for all time inside that ambulance as the green fire blazes beyond the windshield. As will the woman, soon to regain her speech, writing in the man's palm with her finger in the stillness, in the dark. As will my sister who passed on after only two hours in this world, and my young mother who pleaded with her baby, "Don't die, please don't die," until the very end. How far will those souls go—the ones that pooled into a deep orange glow behind the closed lids of my eyes, that enveloped me in that ineffably warm light? How far will the candles travel— the ones lit at the site of every killing, in every time and place laid to waste by unfathomable violence, the ones held by the people who vow never to say goodbye? Will they ride from wick to wick, from heart to heart, on a thread of gold?

In the pamphlet I uncovered in the old shoe box last January, my past self, writing in April of 1979, had asked herself:

Where is love?
What is love?

Whereas, until the autumn of 2021, when *We Do Not Part* was published, I had considered these two problems to be the ones at my core:

> *Why is the world so violent and painful?*
> *And yet how can the world be this beautiful?*

For a long time, I believed that the tension and internal struggle between these sentences was the driving force behind my writing. From my first novel to my most recent one, the questions I had kept in mind continued to shift and unfold, yet these were the only two that remained constant. But two or three years ago, I began to have doubts. Had I really only begun asking myself about love—about the pain that links us—after the Korean publication of *Human Acts* in the spring of 2014? From my earliest novel to my latest, hadn't the deepest layer of my inquiries always been directed towards love? Could it be that love was in fact my life's oldest and most fundamental undertone?

Love is located in a private place called "my heart," the child wrote in April 1979. (*It is inside my thump-thumping beating chest.*) And as for what love was, this was her reply. (*It is the gold thread connecting between our hearts.*)

When I write, I use my body. I use all the sensory details of seeing, of listening, of smelling, of tasting, of experiencing tenderness and warmth and cold and pain, of noticing my heart racing and my body needing food and water, of walking and running, of feeling the wind and rain and snow on my skin, of holding hands. I try to infuse those vivid sensations that I feel as a mortal being with blood coursing through her body into my sentences. As if I am sending out an electric current. And when I sense this current being transmitted to the reader, I am astonished and moved. In these moments I experience again the thread of language that connects us, how my questions are relating with readers through that electric, living thing. I would like to express my deepest gratitude to all those who have connected with me through that thread, as well as to all those who may come to do so.

EVEN IN THE
DARKEST NIGHT

remember the day when I was eight years old.

As I was leaving my afternoon abacus lesson, the skies opened in a sudden downpour. This rain was so fierce that two dozen children wound up huddled under the eaves of the building. Across the street was a similar building, and under those eaves I could see another small crowd—almost like looking into a mirror. Watching that streaming rain, the damp soaking my arms and calves, I suddenly understood. All these people standing with me, shoulder to shoulder, and all those people across the way were living as an "I" in their own right. Each one was seeing this rain, just as I was. This damp on my face, they felt it as well. It was a moment of wonder, this experience of so many different first-person perspectives.

Looking back over the time I have spent reading and writing, I have relived this moment of wonder, again and again. Following the thread of language into the depths of another heart, an encounter with another interior. Taking my most vital, most urgent questions, trusting them to that thread, and sending them out to other selves.

Ever since I was a child, I have wanted to know. The reason we are born. The reason suffering and love exist. These questions have been asked by literature for thousands of years, and continue to be asked today. What is the meaning of our brief stay in this world? How difficult is it for us to remain human, come what may? In the darkest night, there is language that asks what we are made of, that insists on imagining into the first-person perspectives of the people and living beings that inhabit this planet; language that connects us to one another. Literature that deals in this language inevitably holds a kind of body heat. Just as inevitably, the work of reading and writing literature stands in opposition to all acts that destroy life. I would like to share the meaning of this award, which is for literature, with you—standing here in opposition to violence, together. Thank you.

AFTER PUBLICATION

1

The novel has been published.

I don't have to wake up at dawn anymore and light my candle.

I don't have to cover the sensor light on the boiler and unplug the refrigerator, trying to see how bright a candle actually is when a secluded house loses all power. I don't have to pace back and forth, candle in hand, to try to see my shadow, giantlike, surge across the ceiling. I don't have to read the spines of my books, each title rising up in the passing light like a low voice before darkening again—not anymore.

I don't have to clench and unclench fistfuls of snow until my hands grow stiff, trying to make sure

I'll remember how it feels as it melts against skin. I don't have to call a taxi and race to the nearest mountain every time it starts to snow. I don't have to be disappointed when the snow has stopped by the time I reach the foothills. I don't have to stand up from my half-finished bowl of rice and veggies at the local hikers' diner when I see, through the window, that the snow is falling again. I don't have to stray from the trail to enter the trees, to enter the deeper reaches of the forest proper.

I don't have to read source materials anymore. I don't have to type the word "massacre" into my search bar. I don't have to lie under my desk, curled on my side, to try to experience the interior of a hole in the ground. When sunlight streams between the trees lining the road on the hill I pass every day, and the shade beneath their cover seems unusually dark, I don't have to picture corpses there, rotting away.

I don't have to cry.

I don't have to wash my face with tears, not anymore.

I don't have to walk the riverside path, some windy midnight.

I don't have to feel closer to the dead than to the living.

I don't have to give up on this novel, not anymore.

I don't have to wait for the day, someday, when I will be released from this novel. I don't have to keep adding to the list of things I want to do, and things I need to do, once I have my freedom.

2

I grow lighter.

Lighter still.

As if nothing remains inside these bones and skin.

In the darkness before dawn, I think. About my novel, now like a person grown distant. We held each other close, one steadying the other, so determined— but I'm the only one still here.

Then again, who was this "I" to start with?
The person who used to be me back then has already been transformed by this novel; I can no longer return to being that person. So I must ask it differently.
Who am I now? This person, so hollow, stripped bare?

3

I actually read fewer books now than when I was writing the novel. I do less walking, too, and less stretching and strength training. I spend entire afternoons lying down, listening to music. Sometimes I listen to a full cycle of the washing machine from start to finish.

I've already done all the things that were written on my list.

I've met the people I wanted to meet. I've read the things I wanted to read. I've seen the films I wanted to see.

I even went to Seonyudo Park, which I'd been wanting to do, and wandered between the forest and the park structures, reminiscent of ruins.

4

One thought—a resolution—floats to the top.

I can just write again: another novel.

Because that's the only way to be connected again.

But what am I being connected to, through writing? Is it for that, the thing only writing can connect me to, that I have so readied myself, stripping bare? So the current is not interrupted, catching on some bump of the uneven ego?

5

Anyway, routine returns.

Every day I read one book of poetry and one novel, to be recharged by a density of sentences. I stretch and strength-train and walk for two hours a day so I can sit at my desk again for long periods of time.

But after many weeks, having written barely a page, I understand. Writing the next novel now was never going to happen. I had two novellas that I'd been meaning to bind together into a trilogy of snow stories, and it'd been weighing on me that they'd been out there for so long, still separate—so I had decided to whip up a new third novella, to hurry up and make a standalone book. The thing is, it's just so cold. I don't want to freeze, not anymore.

6

Right around this time, as I am giving up, I hear from my publisher. They'd like to make a video introducing the music I listened to while writing *We Do Not Part*. They need me to send the list first, and as I narrow it down to eight or nine songs, I remember a song that I briefly listened to on repeat in January 2019. Its lyrics go like this:

> *I'll rise up*
> *In spite of the ache*
> *I will rise a thousand times again*

The day I first heard this song, I took the back of a calendar sheet, wrote out the numbers 1 to 1,000, and stuck it to the wall. *Let's erase one number per day,* I told myself. *Let's live and write one day at a time; let's just repeat that a thousand times.* This was a thought I had because I'd gone too long without sleeping. I had reached the conclusion that what life I had left held no peace or hope, that everything would only get worse. The strange thing is, the more I worked on the novel, the more I began, gradually, to live. Little by little I could sleep for longer, and over time, the nightmares grew less frequent. How could this be possible, when the novel being written was so full of blood and corpses and bones? It was as I finished the first draft in the fall of 2020, when Kyung-ha lights the match in the final scene, that I understood. This was actually a novel about love. It was a flame melting broken glass back together again, into one whole mass.

7

Nearly seven years passed between the day I wrote the first page of *We Do Not Part* and its completion, making the sheer amount of notes taken along the way considerable. More than ten slim notebooks stand as the record of my groping search for the path forward, questioning and answering myself in turn. There are also versions where I was trying out different characters—and even different narratives—for fifty, a hundred, or even two hundred manuscript pages (the earliest title was *The Night of the Bird's Return*). I open the slim notebook I carried around with me through the winter of 2018, and find the following note jotted inside.

> *Prayer.*
> *A world that barges in.*
> *Is this the world?*
> *Where children are dying and women are*
> *   raped—*
> *Is this the world that has been given to us?*
>
> *And yet, the things that are beautiful for being*
> *   alive.*
> *Relentlessly*
> *Mercilessly beautiful things.*

Ghosts.
Palm trees.
A black tree, waving its arm.

Stories of humans, seeking salvation from this
    nightmarish reality
Horror and violence.
Stories of prayer.

Wind and ocean currents.
The circulation of water and wind
Connecting the entire world.
We are connected to one another.
We are connected,
We must be.

Snow has fallen.
We do not part.
Humans within history.
Humans within the universe.

The sensations of my body.
Flesh. Frail. Mortal.

"I" end up going to that house.
After everyone has left "me."
Become something like a ruin.

The question of just how cold,
How warm,
How hot.

The "I" who wrote about a massacre spends a day
at the house of a friend whose parents survived the
massacre.

The moment, at a certain threshold—living
beings become something more like spirits,
perched at the final edge of profound pain—
when we slip out of our bodies and see, at last,
what lies on the other side.

The finitude of life,
The temporality of existence.
An extremity of meaninglessness.
The flame of time.

I must think on the silence of snow.
Think how snow inhales sound,
How it might inhale "my" own voice, too, and the
sound of birds.

Only snow, at last, once the wind stops.
Only snow, completely noiseless, absorbing all
sound.

This is her house.
The house of a mother who sleeps on a bed of
sawdust
And a father who, tormented by delirium, enters
the mountain each night.

Procession.
All those processions.
American Indians. Auschwitz.

All the massacres.
People without faces.
People turned to pulp.

What I saw that night in Seoul,
Long-haired and slow-paced,
A procession of people, guns in hand.

How many gaps of air does the snow contain?

Crystals.

To die is to grow cold.
For the pile of snow on the face to not melt.
To kill is to make cold.

Dialogue: Walking through the forest I suddenly understood. That I had lived my entire life in the company of ghosts. Even though there was no need. There really was no need to do such a thing. I could have refused you. But I didn't want to refuse. I thought. Let us chip away at them, these ninety-nine spectres of infinite chaos. And let us part—an oath. No, let us do the opposite. Let us never part. An oath.

8

While focusing on writing the second half of this novel in September and October 2020, there was a period when I played music loud enough to make the whole house tremble. I listened to one particular song a great deal: a live concert recording of Kim Kwang-seok's "My Song," performed alone with one guitar and one harmonica. There were a few lines that always shook me up:

> *I may be shaken, I may have fallen, but so long as*
> *This world holds one last drop of water*
> *I will drink it, and sing*

Listening to the music, I would sometimes imagine that I was Kim Yuna, executing something like a spiral. Other times I simply danced, using my whole body. Spinning 'round and 'round, I welled up a few times. I cried, too, my sobs loud.

And then, after, I sat back down at my desk.

   I wrote . . . I wrote.

   Weeping, I wrote.

Not wanting to interrupt the flow, I would eat quickly, standing in the kitchen.

   I even ran to and from the bathroom.

That was me being born again.

   With all my strength, I was coming back to life.

9

When I try to think back on the year and six months before that, which I spent writing *Human Acts,* the first thing that comes to mind is overwhelming pain. To call it a kind of "possession" would, perhaps, make things simpler. To say that I, as a writer, was a medium for a period of time—this would be elegant. But that is not true. Nothing "possessed" me during that time. I did not enter any kind of trance state. At each and every moment, I was clearly in my right mind. Enduring the pain that shattered me, then shattered me again. I looked like a crazy person, I am sure, weeping through gritted teeth in my studio, on the subway, crossing the street, in the kitchen, under my blankets—but the truth is, I wasn't the least bit crazy.

After writing *Human Acts,* I had to think carefully: What had that pain actually been? The pain that readers, too, say they felt along with me? This vivid pain, it is proof of something—but what? Surely not love? Could it be possible that pain stems from love, that this pain was proof of such love? If so, I wanted to write my next novel about that love.

10

The process of writing *We Do Not Part* was much the same. Putting aside the fact that the novel straddles the line between fantasy and reality, I made sure to keep a firm grip on my mind at every moment. Some time ago, during an interview for a bimonthly literary magazine, I found myself sharing a thought I had never spoken aloud before, for fear of just such a misunderstanding. This was likely because of the trust I had in the interviewer, who was a fellow novelist.

Before We Do Not Part *became a novel, what form did it take in your notes?*

A novel that moves from death to life. A novel where people who were half dead are given life. A novel that lights a candle beneath the sea. It's possible that this will sound strange, but . . . there was that incident where a pilot, suffering from depression, committed suicide by crashing a plane, killing a whole lot of other people as well. He died murdering a huge number of living people. So then, couldn't a different person, one who was half dead—in an exact reversal of this airplane incident—bring many who were also dead back with them, all coming back to life together? Of course, in reality, living people are capable of dying, whereas the sequencing of dead people coming back to life is impossible. But couldn't it maybe be possible in some single

45

*given instant? Couldn't someone who had been half
dead, together with these spirits, cross back over into
life, in just one single instant?*

11

If, in the process of writing *We Do Not Part,* I was
granted salvation, that was an incidental outcome
(rather than a conscious goal).

Writing simply pushed me toward life.

All those mornings I greeted with Jeongsim's
heart in my own chest. Living her days, one after the
next; equal parts pain and love, boiling over.

The beating pulse of every moment, unfurling
like wings, like flames.

Inseon's and Kyungha's hands, giving and then receiving the candle, over and over.

12

And if, then, life was passed on to me in this way—a kind of bonus gift with purchase—shouldn't I now harness the force of that life to move forward?

Shouldn't I be writing things that speak of life, while life yet remains?

If permitted, I would like my next novel to set forth from this place.

[2022]

SMALL TEACUP

W hile writing *We Do Not Part,* I made an effort to maintain a few routines. (I did not always succeed.)

1. To wake at five-thirty in the morning and, while my mind was clearest, continue writing the novel from where I had left off the previous day.
2. To walk along the stream near the house I lived in at the time, more than once a day.
3. To steep black tea leaves in the teapot usually used for steeping green tea, and to drink just one cup each time I returned to my desk.

In this way, the act of peering into the bluish interior of this small cup, six or seven times a day, became the center of my life for a time.

*Teacup and message donated to the Nobel Museum in Stockholm (2024)

The Coat and I

I have aged fifty years, and
The coat has aged twenty

Purchased the winter I turned thirty

Sure to last a lifetime, I thought, this long winter
    overcoat
A black coat that covers the calves

A coat with torn lining, and
Stitching along the hem that's burst a few times and
    been sewn back together
With pilling on both cuffs, like little black
Droplets of water, clinging

Here I am, fifty years old,
Putting on this twenty-year-old coat
And strolling out under the winter sun

Hanging on the wall
The coat resembles me, its shoulders bowed
Maybe embracing the
Hollow darkness inside, or
Maybe just leaving it be

Folded in half and draped over a chair
The coat resembles me
Knowing to bend its dusty body low

When I grasp its shoulders to lift it up, grazing the
    floor
It knows to straighten its heavy back

I have aged fifty years, and
The coat has aged twenty

When I stretch out my arm
The sleeve willingly follows

When I raise the collar,
My neck hunches down, sinking into it

When I wear the coat
Does the coat wear me?

The way the outer fabric pulls at the lining
And the lining sheathes the outer fabric

Does the coat embrace me
While I carry it on my back?

I have aged fifty years, and
The coat has aged twenty

Beyond counting,
The things we left, together, the things we
　　embraced,
The things we clung to,
Desperate and tilting, and those
That ultimately slipped away, meanwhile

I have aged fifty years, and
The coat has aged twenty, and now
Fated, someday, to part, embracing and carrying one
　　another
We walk into the winter sunlight

North-Facing Room

Since spring, I have lived in a north-facing room

At first, I was startled at every outing
Discovering, ah, the day is quite bright

By winter I have learned
How to live in this room

Lowering the blinds on the north-facing window,
I turn on only the desk lamp

Once my pupils have gradually opened, my eyes
are dazzled even by faint light

I cannot tell if snow has fallen
If the sun has returned, or simply
Set into an ashy gray dusk

To stop words from melting in the dark
I read the dictionary, little by little

Keep a journal in invisible ink, and it does not seep
    into the desk
I do not record the weather

What was it like, to live in a bright room?
I do not remember, and
I have no wish to go back

Because I have become a north-facing person

Whose light does not change

(Meditation on Pain)

To put a bird to sleep,
They said, cover its cage with a cloth

A black or
Dark-gray cloth
(This thin cloth, in place of night)

In the night, they said, white breast feathers grow,
    swelling
They said, like cotton

Any bird that lies on the metal floor is a dead bird

It waits, they said
Feet curled around its perch
Straight and stiff in the dark
Toes curled tight, blackout

No dreams
Blackout

Remember, to remove the cloth in a timely manner

(It might have wanted to open its eyes,)

Sound(s)

I

Monophony

I awaken
I open my eyes again

To live one more day in this world

Surrounded by screams
Surrounded by moans
Surrounded by eyes flowing with blood

I live one more day

I remember
Our body heat

Smiling

The kinds of things that happen
When we look into each other's eyes
When we clasp our hands together
When we embrace, and stroke the other's back
When we sit quietly in the sun, facing one another

But it is surrounded by screams
Surrounded by moans
Surrounded by wailing cries

That I open my eyes again

To live one more day in this world

||

Biphony

Is there any hope
You asked me

The hope, perhaps, that we can find hope

If something like that can also be called hope
Then I, too, have some hope

If I am nothing more than me
I cannot meet you

If you are nothing more than you
You cannot meet me

I do not, ultimately, live only as myself
Because everything I feel and see, I live out

You do not, ultimately, live only as yourself
Because everything you think and love, you live out

Isn't it strange?
That people we have never once met thicken us

Isn't it frightening?
That layers of time-space we have never actually
traversed make us heavy

Because we are not confined to our height and
weight

Because we swell up
Into billions of layers

Because those billions of layers
Condense and grow firm

Is there any hope
I ask you

We cannot help but imagine hope, so long as we
live—

If something like that can also be called hope, there
is hope

Because we are not confined to our height and
    weight

III

Chorus

Annyeong, in my mother tongue
Is both a first and last greeting

Distinguishable by stress, and intonation, and
    context

Annyeong, nice to meet you.
Annyeong, be well.

Annyeong, we meet again.
Annyeong, let's meet again.

But which is which, it's impossible to distinguish

If there is no stress, no intonation
If not one other word is beside it

If there is no situation
No context

If it is just *annyeong,* a whisper
No more than *annyeong,* a shout

In the beginning, there was a nothingness that flowed

Neither force nor weight, it
Crossed the boundary between immaterial and
    material
To traverse a moment, 10^{-43} seconds, and explode
In a probabilistic instant

After that, we arrived at this point
Growing ever farther apart from each other
Rotating forever

Burning
Cooling
Being sucked in

When the expanding universe reaches its threshold,
Some say, it will contract again into a single point
It will return to flowing nothingness,
Some say, and once again, the probabilistic instant
    will come, exploding past the threshold

Annyeong,
We who both met and parted

Annyeong,
We who have neither met nor parted

Without beginning
Or end
Like a butterfly in flight, spreading and folding its
    wings

This thing we are traversing
This universe—how many times it has contracted,
   and expanded
We cannot know

Annyeong. (Whispering)
Annyeong. (Shouting)

Annyeong, in my mother tongue

Is both a first and last greeting

A Very Small Snowflake

A very small snowflake, you
As if dancing
As if slowly dancing, approach
My face

Instead of falling straight down like all the other
    snowflakes
Somehow, you spread your wings toward my face

But where did you get to, after that?
I never saw you again.

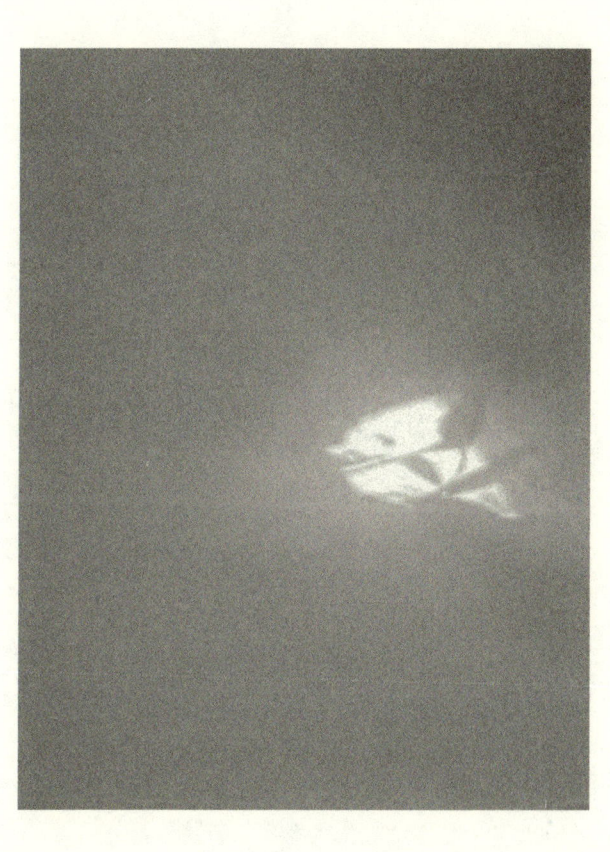

NORTH-FACING GARDEN

Three years ago, in the spring, I bought a ten-*pyeong* house on a fifteen-*pyeong* plot of land. At forty-eight years old, it was the first house I ever fully owned outright, in my own name. I liked that it was on a quiet pedestrian alley, and that it was a single-story house with no tall buildings around to block the sun. More than anything, I liked that the moment I opened the front gate and stepped inside, there was an inexplicably gentle quality to the air, making it feel as if I had entered some small, separate world.

After completing the final payment that summer, I made only the most necessary renovations. Leaving the roof, walls, and pillars intact, I moved the outdoor bathroom indoors. The kitchen plan I sketched out was as compact as the galley in a passenger plane. This was to accommodate the fact that, even after disposing of half my books ahead of the move, there was still nowhere near enough space for what remained. Excluding the one *pyeong* needed to fully open and close the front gate, the courtyard was about four *pyeong,* and to ensure it would receive sufficient sunlight, the flower bed had to be placed right up against the northern wall. Marking out a rectangular plot exactly 180 centimeters long and 40 centimeters wide, I stacked a low ledge of bricks about half a handspan high and filled it with soil. This became the outline of the garden.

What shall I plant, come spring?

As I spent that first winter mulling this over, what came to my mind most often was the scent of lilac. This was thanks to a memory from my college days, when a drift of lilac from the other side of someone's garden wall startled me to a stop as I walked along an alleyway near the university's west gate. The plantain lilies from the yard at the Suyu-ri house came to mind just as often. Each time I saw those white flowers bloom in late August, I would think, *Ah, autumn is coming soon.* I remembered, too, the heavy peony blossoms that would bloom late into the spring, grown from the seeds Mother scattered inside the front gate; and the wooden dais we placed in the shade of the magnolia tree; and looking up into the persimmon tree, counting the red-ripe fruits between branches.

If I could plant a single fruit tree, which would be best? I tried to imagine it. Apricot? Plum? Quince? What about grapes, their vines stretching on and on, endless? Or—though of course, this would mean no fruit—roses, maybe, or trumpet creepers?

With the long-awaited arrival of spring, I arranged for an introduction to a (very youthful-looking) landscaper. A lifelong city person myself, I had no confidence in my own ability to properly plant a tree. Upon meeting the landscaper, who came to the house—This is the smallest work site of my career, he noted—we spoke for an hour and compiled a modest list.

Miss Kim lilac.

Green maple.

Viburnum.

Plantain lily, hosta, and liriope.

The plan: A young green maple currently planted in a corner of the landscaper's own home garden would be transplanted to the center of my flower bed; on either side, leaving an appropriate amount of space in between, would go the Miss Kim lilac and viburnum; and in between these, the shorter hosta and plantain lily and liriope would act as ground cover.

The most important precondition shaping this plan was the fact that the garden faced north. The landscaper discouraged the apricot and quince trees I had wanted, along with the peonies and trumpet creepers and roses; they all needed sunlight.

To plant those things, the plot needs to be bigger. Trees like that need to be right in the middle of the yard, where they can get strong sun.

A few weeks later, the landscaper brought the plants. Digging deep into the soil with a spade, he planted them gingerly, careful not to damage the roots, and then watered them generously with a large watering can—The drainage here is excellent. Very good—before giving me instructions for future care.

No matter how small a garden, it's still a garden,

so it will require a good deal of tending, he warned me, smiling. These guys do well in shade, sure, but if you want them to grow healthy and strong, it can be good to use mirrors.

Mirrors?

He met my surprised echo with an explanation.

To catch the sunlight shining south. By reflecting it. After all, there's no light here, all day long.

To catch the sunlight shining south.

That very night, I ordered three adjustable desk mirrors.

After all, there's no light here, all day long.

I laid these mirrors down at suitable angles to gather the sunlight and send it to the plants; after about a year like that, I ordered three more of the same mirrors. This spring, I ordered another two more, bringing the current total to eight.

I never really knew what sunlight was, before I had this garden.

While I had lived in single-family homes until my late twenties, my room in the Suyu-ri house, where I lived longest, faced north, and even the south-facing living room there was blocked by the two-story house across the yard, leaving no real opportunity to observe the movement of the sun.

After that house, I moved often—so often that if I tried counting with my hands, I'd run out of fingers—always from one kind of apartment to another (eventually I'd lived on every floor between the first and the ninth, all except the sixth; there were some tired moments during those years when I would step into an elevator and suddenly not know which floor to press). Sunlight was like a guest in those multi-unit buildings, making repeated unsatisfying visits, entering through a southeast- or northwest-facing window to perch awkwardly in some patch of balcony or living room or bedroom for a spell, only to disappear behind unyielding concrete walls.

Now I can say I know a bit about sunlight.

Built in the shape of the Korean character ⊏, this house has no external windows that face east. The little study that looks over the inner courtyard, though, does; and the sun shines through that little east-facing window first before striding over to the inside of the front gate to shine through the kitchen window. Every time these slanting streams of noon-day sun spill across the wooden floors, I am startled by the sheer force of their resolute speed.

On days the trees are given their sunlight, I am kept quite busy keeping pace with that speed.

To distribute the light evenly across every tree, the angle and placement of all eight mirrors must be shifted once every fifteen minutes or so. Which was how I came to internalize a sense of the earth's rotation.

Likewise, over time I also came naturally to a sense of the earth's revolution around the sun. Because the angle of the sun changes with the seasons, the placement of each mirror must be shifted, little by little, every three days or so.

When I catch the sunlight with my mirrors and shine them onto the trees, a window of light appears on the white north-facing wall. Inside its frame, the shadows of leaves and branches create forms akin to relief engravings.

There is a translucent pale-green glow produced when sunlight passes through leaves. And there is a specific sensation I feel each time I see it. A sense of joy that feels almost primordial, one I intuit to be inscribed on the human genome, a result of our having lived so long in symbiosis with plants. Enchanted by that joy, I stop writing every fifteen minutes to go out into the yard and adjust the mirrors. I repeat this work until there is no more light to collect.

We're catching the sunlight shining south. By reflecting it with mirrors.

Thus, in my garden there is light.

There are trees that grow, nourished by that light.

Leaves sparkle, translucent, and flowers slowly open.

Over the past three years, I have gradually come to realize that this work is fundamentally transforming my very constitution. As the gentle warmth of this small place holds me close, quiet. With the rhythm of the light changing each day, each moment, each season.

[2022]

GARDEN DIARY

2021

March 21

Because the flower bed is on the north side of the courtyard, I have positioned three mirrors to allow the trees some sunlight. When the southerly noon sun slowly passes these mirrors, a patch of light appears on the wall, like a window.

March 22

The Miss Kim lilac has sprouted all over with light-green leaves. They say an American soldier stationed here during the Korean War took this shrub back home with him, giving it the official name of "Miss Kim," most likely after a woman he had some connection to. Which means that the species of lilac native to Korea is not a tree, but a shrub.

Last week I brought in a cherry bonsai and a blueberry bush, both potted; the cherry blossoms have begun to bloom, and the blueberry flowers are holding buds.

The hosta grows valiantly. All winter it looked as if it had withered to nothing, but then it burst up through the soil, a thing resurrected—and now it is slowly unfurling its leaves, as if finally releasing its grip.

March 23

Last May I planted lilac, viburnum, hosta, and liriope in the flower bed; in June I added a young maple tree and brought in a potted Glossy Abelia. Happily, all the plants survived that summer's record-breaking fifty-four-day rainy season.

March 24

I had scattered some wildflower seeds into three empty pots; three days later they began to sprout, and another two weeks on, they'd grown quite a bit. A friend of the painter K—someone well versed in gardening—had jotted down a list of the seeds for me. Surely they won't all sprout? That was my thought as I scattered all one hundred or so mixed seeds that filled the packet in question, but now they are all coming up so densely that I am starting to worry.

As for which seeds, among the twenty or so listed, have actually sprouted? I will find out when the flowers bloom.

March 25

The blueberry buds were swelling only on the lower branches that had gotten more sunlight, so today I raised the angle of the mirrors. Every day, moment to moment, the light changes.

March 29

The young maple is growing so beautifully that it's actually rather moving. It was much smaller and frailer, in the beginning, than the shrubs to either side, but this year it's grown a bit taller. Of course, it's still as fragile as ever. But in ten years or so it will grow tall and thick enough to reach the eaves. A tree holds such possibility from seed. So long as it does not die. So long as it survives. Eventually, it will grow dense and thick.

March 30

Despite being a kind of hosta, the plantain lily's leaves are much more delicate. They sprout at different times, too, and the shapes of their leaves are different as well. Much softer. More subdued and quiet, in speed and in form.

Of course, I also enjoy the cool vigor of the hosta proper.

April 1

It seemed the garden needed more sun, so I bought three more mirrors. From nine in the morning to three in the afternoon, the sunlight comes in at an angle the mirrors are able to catch—which keeps me very busy, adjusting their position three or four times an hour. Once three P.M. comes around and I am no longer able to bestow sunlight, I sit and quietly look over my shady garden. The garden, filled with (mirrored) light, is . . . so beautiful that it sometimes leaves my chest heavy and aching.

The wildflowers I sowed have continued to grow. What's surprising is that the bracken fern, which I wrote off as completely dead last year, is now thriving and sending up fiddleheads.

April 2

On days when the light is dim, the light of the mirrors grows dim as well. Unable to form a crisp rectangle on the wall, it produces a kind of halo—maybe the souls of the trees.

I heard that tomorrow, it will rain.

April 3

The plantain lily leaves have grown rounded and pretty. The maple leaves are bigger now, too. And the Miss Kim lilac leaves are bigger. (Though they are small leaves still.)

April 4

The viburnum and the maple tree are shooting up as if they are competing against each other. At some point last night, the viburnum grew a little more. It would appear that plants eat sunlight during the day and grow bigger during the night. (Like human children.)

April 6

The blueberry flowers are in bloom.
  The lilac seems ready to bloom soon, too.

April 8

I found another way to use the mirrors and their light. It's about taking the light reflected by the mirror and then reflecting it once more. It makes me happy when the light slants across the leaves—a feeling I assume is now a part of human nature itself, the result of evolution shaping us to live symbiotically with plants.

April 12

Drinking some water, I look at the trees in the court-yard.

Spring has barely arrived and yet here we are, already headed into summer.

April 17

For the first time in two days, I look closely over the garden and see that flowers have bloomed. The little round blueberry flowers look quite a bit like blueberries themselves. The lilac has bloomed white. What surprises me is that the Solomon's Seal I thought had completely died last year has somehow sprouted again, alongside the wildflowers. The resurrection of the bracken fern was similar; I was startled then, too . . . What I have learned is that even if something looks dead above the soil, if its roots are strong, it can come back to life.

April 18

Viburnum branches look like birds. Like they are taking flight.

As for the lilac . . . Why are the blooms still white? Last year they definitely had a lavender cast. Did they not get enough sun?

The plantain lilies have grown thick. Their leaves are round and beautiful. I planted them because I remembered them blooming each August and September back in the house where I lived from age eleven to twenty-five. They bore no flowers last year, but what will this year be like?

There is no way to expand the garden, and so I imagine myself small, shrunk down to the size of a LEGO figure. Then this would be a dense, thick forest—overwhelming.

April 23

1. The lilac has taken on a hint of purple but it is not as deep as last year. I should look into why the color is getting fainter.

2. Once I stopped using the mirrors to reflect light toward the wall, the maple tree started shifting on its own, turning its body toward the center of the courtyard.

3. Purple is appearing on the white blueberry flowers.

4. More little leaves on the bracken fern. I've come to understand why people talk about "pulling (things) up by the root." Roots have power.

April 24

As soon as I opened the gate and walked in yesterday, I looked over the garden—and I could feel the trees suffering. The temperature had risen unexpectedly; they needed more water. I rushed to water them, and by nightfall I could feel their drooping leaves start to come back to life. The forecast for the coming week shows no rain at all. I will have to water them once every three days.

April 25

Yellow flowers have bloomed on the roof.

They were blooming in 2019 as well, but when I worried about them the carpenter said it was fine to leave them be. Weeds that grow too big have to be pulled, he explained, but little ones like these don't cause any harm.

April 26

I completed the novel I have been writing for seven years.

I put the USB stick in the pocket of my jeans and walked all evening.

May 3

The viburnum flower stalks have yet to come up. Elsewhere, viburnums are already in bloom. I look up its flowering season and find that the stalks should have come up ages ago. (In fact, its Korean name, *bulduhwa,* which literally translates to "Buddha's head flower," was chosen because its blooms are fullest around Buddha's birthday.) Possibly it does not plan to bloom at all this year, or it could simply be very late. Either way, you are healthy and lush, I told it inwardly, and that is more than enough. Do whatever you would like to do. (Though of course, such words likely mean nothing to a tree.)

May 11

Aphids have appeared at the tender ends of the viburnum's branches, so I trimmed those parts off entirely. With the growth node cut away, it will have to grow a different branch now if it's to get any taller. Looking into the situation more closely, I learned that viburnum flowers only come into bloom on stalks that are at least two years old. Which means this tree is likely three years old this year. Let's agree to bloom next year, then, and just spend this season growing well.

May 25

The hosta that did not bloom at all last year is putting up four whole flower stalks.

Using a wet tissue, I carefully wipe away the slightly eerie yet prettily named white pests known as "fairy bugs" I find on the viburnum branches. (Luckily, they say these are not particularly dangerous, so the branches can stay.) While engaged in this task, I see a fly narrowly escape getting caught up in a spider's web. The viburnum and the maple tree and the lilac bush are all invading one another's territories, struggling to claim more sunlight.

May 31

The viburnum sprawled so furiously outward that it covered the maple leaves, so I gathered it together with a bit of twine.

The sunlight is good, the sky very blue.

June 3

The blueberry leaves grew so densely that they blocked the maple tree and failed to bear any actual fruit, so I pruned its branches a bit. Should I have wielded my shears more boldly? I will try again, when my heart has grown tougher.

June 5

Just now, a sparrow strolled around between two of the flowerpots before flying up onto the roof and disappearing. I thought it was a mouse at first, and put on my glasses in a total panic—only to see a truly lovely little bird. There was a butterfly in here, too, just a few days ago.

June 6

Because the height of the noon sun gradually gets higher and higher, I am constantly having to change the position of the mirrors. A day or two is fine, but any longer than that and the mirrors can no longer carry out their intended function. The earth rotates and revolves faster than I ever thought.

Raising plants, one hopes only that they will grow and thrive. There is no expectation of mutual interaction. No need for jokes or wit or thanks, no warm words. All they need to do is be well.

June 7

The hosta flowers are blooming. These splendid flowers are the reason for the butterflies and bees.

As I tie the viburnum with more twine so it does not grow flat against the ground, raindrops begin to fall—and I glimpse, just then, the astonishing, eerie sight of a fairy bug crawling along, its body like pure white cotton. I catch it, quick, and put it in a plastic bag . . . and ah, I think I can see why they call these fairy bugs. They actually don't look like insects at all. They don't even look like living creatures, really, or anything else from this world. And yet here they are, crawling around and eating plants!

June 10

I discovered four fairy bugs and brushed them away
with a wet wipe. Spotting another that had camou-
flaged itself against the white wall, I moved to catch
it . . . only to have it suddenly launch into the air.
Fairy bugs can fly!

June 11

When I see the lilac grow faster than the maple tree, spreading its vines, vigorously and without hesitation, over and across the maple's leaves—I am overcome with an urge to protect the maple tree. Like a home-room teacher watching over the most introverted child in their class.

June 12

One hosta flower has come fully into bloom.

Two sparrows that had been up on the roof came down into the courtyard and perched on the maple awhile before leaving again. They even walked a few steps around the potted blueberry bush. I felt proud, somehow, that these birds had judged the house worth visiting. When I first heard a noise up on the roof, I started and looked up—it was coming from a direction from which no sound could come. Hail, maybe, or some sort of stone dust? But then a pretty bird head popped out from the tin gutter. I felt I shouldn't make any sound myself, so I kept very still and watched, quiet.

June 20

The Glossy Abelia has bloomed. It normally blooms in May, so the fact that it is blooming now has to mean the courtyard really doesn't get enough light. The cherries stopped ripening halfway, and the blueberries bore not a single fruit. What the landscaper said back when we were making our list of trees was true: No fruit trees. It's a north-facing garden. Still, at least the flowers bloom.

June 22

Spots have appeared on the viburnum's leaves, like flecks of white paint. What can it be? I had been gone a few days, and I was checking to make sure the fairy bugs weren't back when I noticed the spots.

I sent a photo to the landscaper; he replied that they were mites. He tells me to spray them with a pesticide. If I leave them be, he says, the leaves will dry up. The viburnum, I am learning, grows fast, and is much harassed by bugs.

June 23

Yesterday I went to the pharmacy and purchased a low-toxicity pesticide—claimed to be less harmful to humans, and even safe to spray on one's pets—then came home and sprayed it on the backs of the viburnum leaves. I had prepared myself, in my way, for the task, wearing a mask, rubber gloves, and rubber boots, but it was still my first time—and with no know-how to speak of, I ended up getting the stuff in my hair and on my forehead. Hardest of all, though, was having no way to know whether I was actually doing it properly.

On one side of the tree, quite a few dried-up leaves had already fallen, tortured by mites, and even the leaves still on their branches fluttered lifelessly to the ground the second my hand grazed them. Seeing this, I understood that this was not a simple problem. I also understood why the landscaper had said, "Well, it's mite season. I'm battling my own mites right now as well." I took a shower, laundered all the clothes I'd worn while spraying, and headed out so as not to be late for my next appointment.

When the skies opened up in a sudden afternoon downpour, I happily pictured all the pesticides being washed away, soaking into the ground, and hoped all the mites would disappear right along with them. But then the next morning, when I stepped into the courtyard, all the many spiders usually in residence had disappeared. The flies and roly-poly bugs, too, and even the ants—all gone. A chilly, frightened feeling. A lonesome feeling.

June 25

The viburnum leaves. Thanks to the mites, the once dense and luxuriant summer leaves have all thinned as if it were early spring. The pesticide I sprayed so clumsily has left scars on what leaves remain. Will it survive? Will it ever grow thick again? The garden, meanwhile, is as quiet as ever. Not even an insect to be heard.

July 25

In the meantime, the maple tree and lilac bush have both grown considerably. The viburnum is barely hanging on. A branch of Glossy Abelia, growing seemingly without limit, sparkles in the sunlight.

Now, 32 degrees Celsius feels nice and cool.

(After writing this, I checked and found that it is actually 34 degrees Celsius.)

August 22

I need to record what happened with the mites.
Before all the viburnum leaves that were attacked
by the mites withered and fell (they say if all the
leaves fall at once, the tree dies), I sprayed the back
of every leaf with pesticide again, one at a time. It
seems a few surviving mites fled the pesticide-coated
viburnum and moved to the blueberry and cherry
plum pots; in the few days I was away, their leaves
had been withered to a crisp brown. With no idea
what to do, I set those two pots outside the front
gate. But that night, when I returned with two
seventy-five-liter garbage bags, one for each pot, they
were both gone. The district sanitation department
had mistaken them for recyclables and taken them
away.

And so, like that, the courtyard was simplified. Its little ecosystem had essentially experienced a cycle of epidemic, quarantine, and eradication. I no longer want to bring in any potted plants. I would simply like to take good care of the plants I already have.

August 24

This year, again, the hosta did not bloom.

I did my best to pay attention, with all the mirrors and the reflected light, but it was not enough.

September 5

The book has come out, so for several days I had no time at all to check in on the garden.

Taking a quick look as I wait for a taxi to Paju, I count five maple leaves, ripened to red.

October 13

Every day, I learn how the angle of the light changes in autumn.

I adjust the position of the mirrors accordingly, a little at a time.

November 6

The leaves are all turning.

November 15

Starting in October, the angle of the sunlight would not reach the mirrors, no matter what I did—so the trees were left in shade around the clock. The sun simply came in lower, stretching longer, until in November it began to reflect off the glass doors of the living area to reach the undersides of the trees. When I think back on last February, I remember the sunlight lying even deeper, stretching all the way to the inner reaches of the living area, while the light reflecting off the glass windows shone fully on the flower bed.

December 18

In the scene set by my little house, there is no out-side world. The tranquility bestowed by a courtyard. A courtyard reminiscent of one's interior landscape.

No passersby, no street, no chance moments.
To avoid forgetting these things completely, one must regularly go out the front gate.

But even in this introverted house, there are direc-tions that open outward. The sky above the court-yard. I watched the snow falling from that sky for a long while.

December 19

I listen to the sound of snow, piled on the roof tiles, melting and trickling down the gutter.

It sounds like music.

2022

April 12

This is my first garden diary entry since the start of the new year.

A few days ago I sprayed eco-friendly pesticide on each of the hundred or so aphids covering the maple tree, one by one. I found myself worrying: What if I missed an aphid or two? What if, thanks to all this time, every one of my trees is now covered in aphids? Imagining the worst-case scenario, I purchased another pesticide at the pharmacy, but when I finally entered, opening that front gate after days away, all—*astonishing*—was well. Quietly, every tree simply put forth its leaves.

April 21

Little house.
     Growing trees.

May 19

Meanwhile, I have trimmed away two viburnum branches that were covered with aphids, and sprayed pesticide on the branches that had only a few. I resent the aphids, the way they focus all their attacks on the tender baby leaves. This pest damage over the last two years seems to be why the viburnum flowers have not bloomed this year, either.

July 29

I have learned that lack of water is the reason aphids and mites appear on plants, so I gave them plenty of water.

The lilac has grown the most this summer. I have been told lilac can grow as tall as three meters, so I shall wait and see.

October 7

This morning I had the water meter checked and the septic tank cleaned. I was sweeping the courtyard, the front gate thrown wide open, when they both arrived at practically the same time, completed their tasks in a blink, and left. I had some flowerpots on the septic tank cover, so I moved them out of the way in advance—but this new spot they're in actually isn't bad at all, and I am thinking of leaving them there for the time being.

I look up at the sky from the courtyard, and a flock of geese is flying past in the shape of the letter ㅅ.

October 10

As I left the house, I heard myself say, "Be right back."
The house feels like a friend.

November 2

In winter, a south-facing house becomes a jar of light.

November 30

While wrapping the garden faucet with an old coat to keep it from freezing, my hands ended up frozen. I was struck by how much the lilac around the faucet had grown.

December 2

Yesterday Mother came to this house for the first time. Until now, the pandemic had forced her to simply sit with her curiosity—but attending the award ceremony became an occasion for her to finally make the trip. Going to meet her at Yongsan Station, I bought a thick, padded jacket; I was sure she wouldn't be dressed properly for the cold. I put it on her first thing, the moment we met on the platform. As we opened the front gate and stepped into the courtyard, she asked:

My word, what are all these mirrors?

Once she was inside, looking out into the courtyard, she said:

This reminds me so much of the house where you were born.

The size of it?

The size, yes, and also the courtyard. It feels exactly the same.

My earliest memories take place in the house I lived in around age four. There are no traces left of the very first house I lived in for the three years before that, not in my memory and not in any photograph. Is it only now, then, that I am learning the reason I fell in love the moment I first stepped into this house? The reason why time spent here gives off a kind of gentle warmth, impossible to describe?

Mother refused to let me brew any tea, saying it was far too drafty and cold. (*You have to get new windows, how can anyone live in a house where the wind just comes right in like this? Later on, when you have the means, be sure to buy a proper apartment. And throw out all those junky mirrors. And sweep these leaves while you're at it.*) Lying down together, face-to-face and holding hands under a shared blanket, we chatted about this and that until it was time to go to the ceremony.

2023

March 20

The viburnum's leaves are unfurling apace, one day to the next.

March 27

The viburnum flowers are blooming this year!
I have counted seven blossoms in all.

I have a feeling the lilacs will bloom soon, too.

March 30

I had been wanting to fill the north wall full of green, and now time is doing the job for me.

April 15

How wondrous, the viburnum. It has grown taller than I am.

May 1

When I step through the front gate, the scent of lilac
is everywhere.

HAVING MANAGED
TO LIVE SOME MORE

Having managed to live some more
Will I be able to think, in the moment before
    death—

I have held life close, tight in my arms.
(Through writing.)

I met people.
Very deeply. Intensely.
(Through writing.)

I managed to live enough.
(Through writing.)

Sunlight.
I looked at the sunlight a long time.

사랑이란 어디있을까?
팔딱팔딱 뛰는 나의가슴 속에 있지.

사랑이란 무멀까?
우리의가슴과 가슴사이을 연결해 주는
아름다운 금실이지.

Where is love?
It is inside my thump-thumping beating chest.

What is love?
It is the gold thread connecting between our hearts.

About the Author

HAN KANG was born in 1970 in South Korea. She is the author of *The Vegetarian,* winner of the International Booker Prize; *Human Acts; The White Book; Greek Lessons;* and *We Do Not Part.* In 2024, she was awarded the Nobel Prize in Literature.

han-kang.net

About the Translators

MAYA WEST was born and raised in Korea. She has an MFA in prose from the University of Michigan and operates an independent project space in Seoul called SALT.

E. YAEWON translates from and into Korean. Recent translations include works by Hwang Jungeun and Maggie Nelson. She is also co-translator, with Deborah Smith, of Han Kang's *Greek Lessons*.

PAIGE ANIYAH MORRIS translates from Korean. Recent translations include Heuijung Hur's *Failed Summer Vacation* and her co-translation with e. yaewon of Han Kang's *We Do Not Part*.